I0504003

THE BUSINESS

MINDSET

Unlocking Your Potential One

Chapter at a Time

BY

MON DE LESEO WILLIAMS

Copyright Notice

© Mon De Leseo Williams

All rights reserved. No part of this publication may
be reproduced, distributed, or transmitted in any form
or by any means, including photocopying, recording,
or other electronic or mechanical methods without
the prior written permission of the publisher, except
in the case of brief quotations embodied in critical
reviews and certain other noncommercial uses
permitted by copyright law. For permission requests,
please contact the publisher.

mwtheauthor@gmail.com

www.mwtheauthor.com

TABLE OF CONTENT

INTRODUCTION

In this book, you will obtain the keys to unlocking your business dreams. It will guide you through the ways to produce your best work at the quickest rate, how to respond to failure, and how to grow from it as well as many other helpful tips.

This book contains some hard lessons that will make you the best at your business, whatever your business may be. Through eleven chapters of simple yet intense advice, you will come away with the mental attitude that is required to run a top-quality business.

Each chapter comes with an activity. It is up to you whether you do them, but I highly recommend it because they give your brain the time to absorb the information and truly take it on board. This book offers you the tools, but true success is up to you.

ACKNOWLEDGEMENT

I would like to give a special thank you to God and

my team.

CHAPTER ONE

HOW TO START A BUSINESS

"A small business is an amazing way to serve and leave an impact on the world you live in."– Nicole Snow (CEO of Darn Good Yarn).

Converse with any entrepreneur, and you will hear different advice across the business world. But the truth is that starting a business is easy and straightforward. Do not be discouraged. A thought cannot become a business without exertion.

If you are willing to put in a little effort to build a business, the payoff will gradually show. To get started you are going to want to know the right steps to take.

As opposed to wasting your time and speculating where to begin, follow this six-point checklist to transform your business from a light bulb over your head to genuine substance.

The six-point business start-up checklist include the following:

1.   Refine your idea and come up with a name.

You likely as of now have a thought of what kind of business you want to start. If not, come up with something that you feel will make a lot of revenue but at the same time be something you are interested in. Then search for existing businesses in your chosen industry. Realize what they have to offer and see how you can improve on what they are doing.

2.   Determine your legal business structure.

A Limited Liability Company (LLC) is recommended because it protects your personal assets by limiting the liability to the resources of the business itself. An LLC has its own added tax benefit.

3.   Register with the government and Internal Revenue Service (IRS).

The IRS requires all businesses to acquire an Employer Identification Number (EIN), which is comparable to a Social Security Number. This is the number used to identify a business and can acquired by completing an IRS form.

One of the primary aspects of starting a business enterprise is registering it. Primarily, a business is registered with the state in which it operates. Registering your business with the Secretary of State entities helps you start and run your business legally.

4.   Brand yourself and advertise.

Branding is one of the most significant parts of any business, large or small. An effective brand strategy gives you a major edge in progressively competitive markets. But what exactly does "branding" mean? How can it influence a private venture like yours?

Simply put, your brand is your promise to your customer. It tells them what they can expect from your products and services, and it differentiates your offerings from your competitors'. Your brand is your image, and it comes from what your identity is, what you need to be, and what individuals see you to be.

5.   Grow your business.

There are many ways to grow your business: Get out, network and exchange business cards, make and distribute flyers, use social media to your advantage and get word out, give back to the community in the name of your business. There is so much you can do to give your business that exposure.

6.   Build your team.

"You don't build a business, you build people, and then people build the business."– Zig Ziglar (American author, salesman, and motivational speaker)

Comprehend the qualities of every person; almost certainly, your new team will have originated from an assortment of foundations. It's important to recognize this because understanding people is worth its weight in gold. If you can enable each employee to channel their strengths and shine in a way that benefits your business, then you are on the right track.

"High expectations are the key to everything."– Sam Walton (founded Wal-Mart and Sam's Club).

Activity

We have discussed the six-point business start-up checklist to start a business. The first paramount step in any journey is clear comprehension of the road ahead and the mission to embark on the journey (purpose). Use each discussed point for a successful business start-up.

1. Get familiar with each point and ruminate on how you can use them for your business.

2. Try to seek opinions from business owners on mastering each point.

CHAPTER TWO
DO SOMETHING PRODUCTIVE

You might be wondering what the next step is to achieve your dream. Like everything, you form the beginning with solid actions, repeated until they become habits. Habitual actions are the key to productive behaviors. Not only do they create patterns of good behavior, but they also build productive habits that let us have more energy to make big business decisions. This snowballs into more power.

As Octavia Butler (American science fiction author) once said, "Habit is more dependable. Habit will sustain you whether you're inspired or not. Habit will help you finish and polish your stories. Inspiration won't."

Doing something meaningful each day is the best way to start moving toward the things that you want. Whether in love or business, it is the small impacts that cause big ripples. Like a tiny raindrop in the ocean, that tiny influence causes widespread ripples, and these ripples are where we find our success.

"Simplicity boils down to two steps: Identify the essential. Eliminate the rest. -Leo Babauta (Author, Vegan and Minimalist).

Like attracts like, and if you want to be successful, you need a successful approach to your day. But what does this mean? Put simply, it means that you need to get up and do something about the things that you want. Be proactive; be preemptive; be productive.

For some people this could be as easy as creating a list and checking things off. How is not the issue; the issue is getting it done. Success is built on a foundation of little actions. Consider these small actions to be small art pieces that will look like a glorious Roman mosaic when completed. Alone, they might be mere pieces, but together they build a magnificent result. When starting out you don't need to have the whole mosaic, but you do need to have a piece to lay down to make a start.

"It is not enough to be busy, so are the ants. The question is: What are we busy about?" -Henry David Thoreau (American essayist, poet, and philosopher).

The pieces you will need to implement will vary with the project you are taking on but identifying these is easy. There are a few that regularly come up. Some ideas are as follows:

- Create a post on social media showing the latest products or services you have to offer (or start a business account if you don't have one for your brand).

- Start a business plan to map out your plans and implement your next steps in your business. The easiest way is to pay a professional to write it for you.

- Educate yourself on business taxes and business terms. Look into getting an accountant to help you keep track of your finances.

- Research market changes and trends in your line of business to make sure that your company stays relevant and offers the best value and customer service.

- Market your product. You can do this through newspapers, online avenues, putting up flyers, encouraging word of mouth, and so on.

- Do some market research to keep up to date on customer needs in your field of work and create a buyer persona [model that describes your typical or target customer based on detailed audience research].

- Write a blog post or find someone to feature you on their blog to get your business out there.

- Write down what setup tasks you need to complete for your upcoming projects.

- Write a list of goals and map out how you will achieve them.

- Read books, magazines, and blogs about your business.

- Figure out a basic work schedule for every day and stick to it.

- Write a Strengths, Weaknesses, Opportunities, and Threats (SWOT) analysis.

You don't have to do these things all at once. In fact, doing things too quickly will most likely cause you to be counterproductive. To be productive and get into the habit of productivity, you should be completing a few tasks a week or even one task a week. This may seem overwhelming, but it is a must for success. Each day you must do something, *anything*, productive, even if it is a small task. If you're writing a book, make sure you write a chapter a week. If you're advertising, make one social media post marketing your product. If you're writing a budget, do the first few steps. One productive accomplishment a day will ensure your future success.

You might be asking how this tiny task approach could possibly be productive. Doing something is better than doing nothing. Buddha once said that a drop a day fills a cup.

This is exactly the case here. You can't fill a cup with nothing, but something added daily *will* fill it eventually. Obviously, this isn't the quickest way to succeed in your business. This act is less about overnight success and more about the productive pattern you form. These patterns are the droplets that go on to making those big changes that will turn you into a tycoon.

This is all well and good to read, but you must implement these strategies into your life. Probably by now you have a few ideas buzzing around in your head. After all, that's why you embarked on this journey, right? You wanted to make things happen. You had an idea and a dream, but either you couldn't start them because the whole process overwhelmed you, or you didn't know how to start. That's why we're going to talk about ways to get started and be productive during your day. Before that, you need to absorb one, simple mantra.

Stop making excuses.

These are three simple words that, in some time in our lives, we all need to hear.

Stop. Making. Excuses.

Let that sink in.

It might seem simple. It's not. Most of you reading this will say, "I don't make excuses. I genuinely have to–" No. The only thing that you genuinely need to do is act like you want this. I know that you want this. You wouldn't be reading this book if you didn't.

Good things come to those who *work*. You need to stop making excuses and start making time.

Do you think that J. K. Rowling was privileged enough to write Harry Potter as her full-time job? Absolutely not! She was a single mother working at Amnesty International and writing on napkins when she went to get coffee. You have the time; you need to find it and carve out a section of your life to work on it. Even if you work a twelve-hour shift, there are options and things you can do. You could prep your meals for a whole week on Sunday or eat something that takes only a few minutes in a convection oven to warm up. Every second is important. And when you're commuting, try listening to affirmations to keep your spirits up.

It's about how much you want this. Are you willing to make sacrifices? Are you ready to take risks? Are you following your dreams?

Perhaps the most important question is: Are you being productive?

"Life is too complicated not to be orderly." - Martha Stewart (American retail businesswoman, writer, television personality, and former model).

Remember the power of P!

Productivity, Passion, Pro-activeness, Patience, Performance

You are the only person who can accomplish your dreams. Stop relying on others and stop making excuses. Go do it.

Overall, success is hard to define, so you need to define it by your own standard—and then you need to raise the bar. It might take some time, but only you can achieve the things you dream of. It is your journey, and you are the one responsible for making it happen.

Get things done—no excuses.

The buyer persona template is for market research and surveys to keep up to date on customer needs in an industry.

USER PERSONA

TEMPLATE

The foundation of any good digital marketing campaign starts with a simple question: How well do I know my customers?

Knowing your target market will help you understand who you want to attract and focus your marketing messages to get in front of those who are most likely to buy your product or service.

That's why you need a buyer persona—a fictional representation of your ideal customer.

Use this template to create your user personas by following the instructions from lesson "How to Create Your Buyer Personas and User Journeys."

User Persona	
Name	
Current Situation	
Desired outcome	
Struggles and painpoints	

Key Takeaways

- You can achieve productivity one small action at a time.

- The ongoing effect is always greater than the initial action.

- Forming good habits is crucial.

- Productivity, big or small, is the foundation for success.

- **Don't make excuses!**

- Make time for the things you need to work on.

- You are the basis of your destiny—nobody else.

- Doing nothing gets you nothing.

- Productive habits get results.

"The journey of a thousand miles begins with one step."– Lao Tzu (ancient Chinese philosopher and writer).

Activity

So, you've come to the end of the chapter, and you're all fired up. You are ready to get proactive about your business. I'm sure that you are excited to dive right in but reading without application can be a form of procrastination, and that's one P that will stop things happening for you. So, before you move on, take a few minutes for this activity.

1. Take a piece of paper or use the note function on your phone and write/type what you want for your business—in a few words. Make it clear and concise.

2. Underneath this, write/type three steps that you are going to take to achieve these goals.

3. Now put it somewhere that you will see it every day—on the fridge, on your vision board, on your phone's wallpaper, or on the dashboard in your car to name a few places. Then, you can move on to the next chapter.

CHAPTER THREE
SET GOALS AND MAP THEM

You've got this far in the book, so I know that you are committed to your goal. Let's look at turning that dream into a reality.

One of the major differences between those who want and those who do is planning. Anyone can have a goal, but only those who act upon it will ever achieve success. Everyone wants to be rich, but no one wants to work hard for it.

To do this you need to map each one of those dreams out.

There are many ways to map out a goal. You can use a Kanban board, vision board, spreadsheet, or any of the numerous apps that you can download. This is completely up to you. For now, though, we are going to discuss the components you need to map out. These do not change with whichever method you choose, and each is an integral cog in the machine of your success.

First, write down your goal. This could be something as simple as "Improve profits by 5%" or "Raise social media followership to 1,000." The details do not matter at this point. The goal is the end of the map, and it is better to work backward, tackling each step along the way.

Moving backward, you need to address the major things that need to change to reach this goal. Again, you don't need much detail here. This is your method of transport to the goal. For this chapter let's use the example of improving a photography business. Improving the business is the goal. The mode of transport, or method of attainment, could be something like **getting better equipment**, **increasing exposure**, and **increasing sales**. As you can see the specifics are not yet important. You need to break down the goal into smaller categories. I recommend focusing on a maximum of five goals; anything more and things get too congested and complex. Less than five goals are completely acceptable, and in fact, having two or three yields the best results.

- So where are we at with the journey now?
- We have decided where we're going to go: the goal.
- We have decided the method of transport, aka, how to get there: the categories.

Now it is time to look more in depth at the root. First, you must assess your starting point. You cannot begin a journey without knowing where you currently are. Gather information on your business: Which other big businesses exist that deal in your line of work, and what are their business models? Take tips from them. What are the trending topics when it comes to products in your business category?

And what can you do to stand out differently from the competition?

Having this information allows you to see what stops you will need to take. Like taking an intercity bus, you will have to plan ahead which buses to take get you to your final destination. This is what it takes to get from step to step to reach your final goal. You *need* to address this to progress.

Let's use the photography business example again; one of the categories that we chose was **getting better equipment**. Here you will need to write a list of what steps to take. This is where detail comes into play.

Consider these:

- Do some market research on what your competitors are using.

- Do some industry research on the latest technology that will give you an edge over the competition.

- Determine how much the equipment you want costs.

- Figure out how many jobs you will have to complete to get enough money to purchase the equipment.

- Purchase the equipment.

This may seem like a long and drawn-out way of thinking of things, but using a list has many benefits, particularly in larger projects. Not only do they keep you from missing items, having lists allow you to manage your time more appropriately.

Another category was **increasing exposure** to the photography business. You could share a short video of your new piece of equipment on YouTube, write a comparative blog for other people interested in photography or the new equipment you purchased, or have a raffle to raise money and have a drawing where the top three people win free photo sessions.

The last thing on the list was to **increase sales**. There are many ways to do this, but increasing exposure will most certainly increase your sales, especially when you have upgraded your equipment. This completes all the categories that we mapped out to improve the photography business.

A more systematic approach would be to use SMART goals. SMART is an acronym you can use to guide your goal setting.

SMART goals consist of five elements:

1. **Specific**

The goal should be clear and specific.

Try to answer these five questions:

- What do I want to accomplish?

- Why is this goal important?

- Who is involved?

- Where is it located?

- Which resources or limits are involved?

Example

Getting better equipment will enable me to take better-quality pictures.

2. Measurable

You need to have measurable goals to accurately track your progress and stay motivated.

A measurable goal should address these questions:

- How much?

- How many?

- How will I know when it is accomplished?

Example

I will only need one upgraded camera to make this happen.

3. Attainable

Goal needs to be achievable and realistic to be a success. It should challenge you but still be attainable.

An achievable goal will answer these questions:

- How can I accomplish this goal?

- How realistic is the goal based on other constraints, such as financial factors?

Example

In my current state I do not have enough money to get the camera, but if I work hard and get more clients, I will be able to buy the new camera in no time.

4. **Relevant**

The goal should be in accordance with other relevant goals, and this step ensures the goal matters to you. Relevant goals will have you answer "yes" to these questions:

- Does this seem worthwhile?

- Is this the right time?

- Does this match our other efforts or needs?

- Am I the right person to reach this goal?

- Is it applicable in the current socioeconomic environment?

Example

I am the right person to reach this goal because taking this step will ensure I keep the clients I have, and they will surely refer their friends and families.

5. **Time-Bound**

In conclusion, setting a timeframe for your goal gives you something to look forward to. It gives you a deadline and helps keep your focus on track. Time-bound goals will answer these questions:

- When?

- What can I do six months from now?

- What can I do six weeks from now?

- What can I do today?

Example

Seeing as this task does not require much effort other than saving money, I will set a deadline of six months from now.

"Our goals can only be reached through a vehicle of a plan, in which we must fervently believe, and upon which we must vigorously act. There is no other route to success." – Pablo Picasso (Spanish painter, sculptor, printmaker, ceramicist, and theatre designer).

Activity

This activity is designed to assist you with your planning steps. Answer the questions briefly for a and b and then in as much detail as you can for c.

a) Pick a goal for your business.

b) What smaller goals (categories) will help you get there? Pick up to three and no more than five.

c) What are the tasks that will help you achieve the smaller goals (categories)?

CHAPTER FOUR
PAY YOURSELF FIRST

"A cardinal rule in budgeting and saving is to pay yourself first. Once your paycheck hits your account, wisdom has it that you should move some amount to savings/investment even before you pay the bills." - John Rampton (entrepreneur, investor, online marketing guru, and startup enthusiast).

Economists define human needs to be insatiable. This means that irrespective of the amount we earn or make daily, our needs will still be far greater than what our income is. Whenever we receive a paycheck, it is tempting to spend the money almost immediately on bills, groceries, gadgets, and other things. However, like Robert Kiyosaki admonished us in one of his top-selling books, *Rich Dad, Poor Dad*, we should pay ourselves before indulging in any expense. The idea is to get your money to increase exponentially via passive income in such a way that you can use the returns from that investment to finance your needs and wants.

FAMILY BANK

Let us say you in your early thirties with good health. You have a $750 car payment per month: $750 x 12 = $9,000.

In one year, $3,000 goes to interest and $6,000 goes to principal on a $30,000 vehicle you financed.

So, $3,000 X 5 = $15,000 in interest to pay the car off; you spent $45,000 total and cannot get that back. Now let us use the same money that you made in five years and put it into a whole life insurance plan that accrues cash value over time.

So, $750 a month into a whole life insurance plan x 12 months = $9,000 invested. After the same five years you will have invested $45,000 into your life insurance plan!

You can borrow money against the plan and start a family bank.

If you were to die, the whole life insurance plan would deduct what you owe and pay the rest to your family (death benefit).

You should get a whole life insurance plan for your children, whenever they are first born. By the time they reach adulthood, they will have money accrued to give them a big head start in life.

Stop paying your bills out of your savings or checking account and going broke each month, giving your interest to loan companies and so on.

BECOME YOUR OWN BANK!

How Do I Pay Myself First?

Paying yourself first simply means that whenever you get paid, before paying any expense that will not yield profits or returns in the future, you save or invest first. Invest in yourself by investing in the stock market, putting money into your 401(k), a Roth IRA (Individual Retirement Account), a savings account, or a product, and so on. The first bill you pay each month (or anytime you receive payment) should be to yourself.

What this means is that you need to hold off on paying any bill to pay yourself first and keep your money working. Hopefully, you will *double* your money *and* be able to pay the bill *and* any late fees *and* have extra money in your pocket.

It is good we all understand that banks feast on our savings. Although they lend these savings to their customers and charge huge interest rates (as high as 26% per annum), they give the savings account holders a meager interest in return (as low as 1.5% per annum). This is how banks make use of clients' money to make reinvestments and how they can afford interest payments to you, the customer.

The problem with keeping too much money in the bank is that when you do not invest, you are effectively losing out on money because your money is sitting there barely collecting interest. Once you have socked away enough money to *six months to a year of living expenses*, you should not continue to put your spare cash in the bank. Also, save up additional cash, stash it away in a safe, and put a rubber band around every $5,000 you make.

"It's not how much money you make, but how much money you keep, how hard it works for you, and how many generations you keep it for." – Robert Kiyosaki (American businessman and author).

Having understood how unwise it is to have *all* your money in a savings account, we will discuss investments and investment options. Whenever you invest, you put a sum of money into a business or use it to buy an asset that can yield multiple returns over time. Imagine what your worth would have been by now if you had invested in huge companies like Apple, Disney, Starbucks, or McDonald's many years ago (when they were still start-ups). You wouldn't have to work another day in your life (although entrepreneurs should never cease from making another dollar). These are returns you would never get by merely putting your money into a savings account.

"Be fearful when others are greedy and be greedy when others are fearful."– Warren Buffet (American investor, business tycoon, philanthropist, and CEO and chairman at Berkshire Hathaway)

Another way to invest is to study, find your niche, and undergo a solid assessment. Then you can begin studying past and future trends. Once you are satisfied, you can make your investment.

You should start small, even though making long-term investments is better than making short-term investments, according to Warren Buffet. One thing about investments that makes it unique from some saving accounts is that you are not penalized for making withdrawals or cashing out.

"Ninety percent of all millionaires become so through owning real estate. More money has been made in real estate than in all industrial investments combined. The wise young man or wage earner of today invests his money in real estate." -Andrew Carnegie (Scottish American industrialist and philanthropist).

More than 400,000 Americans are homeless with about 70% of all extremely low-income families paying more than half their income on rent. This identifies the housing issues we have in the United States. If you have the money to begin real estate acquisition, now is the right time. You will have an income for life. This income snowballs, allowing you to purchase more properties. People will always need places to rest their heads.

Additionally, you can also purchase investment pieces such as gold. Investing in gold requires being a bit informed about the product; however, if you are quite knowledgeable about the subject, the rewards far outweigh the risk.

It is important to manage your bills carefully; however, it is much more important to be diligent and resourceful by making investments and looking for the best options available.

Pay Yourself Checklist

- Get a credit card or switch your existing credit card to one that offers 0% APR (annual percentage rate).

- Write a schedule of when you need to make credit card payments and try to pay a little before the due date (to boost your credit score quickly).

- Buy something small on a credit card then pay it off quickly.

- Shop around regularly to find the most competitive deals, especially those deals that meet a regular need.

- Start a family bank.

- Buy into stocks, shares, or bonds and try to invest monthly.

- Look into Forex Trading (Foreign Exchange Market that is a global marketplace for exchanging national currencies against one another).

- Reduce bills by canceling any unnecessary ones.

- Claim any tax-deductible expenses.

- Ask your phone or Internet service providers for occasional discounts.

- Study what investment pieces to buy.

- Purchase investment pieces.

- Study stock trends and keep up to date with past and future market trends.

- Read books and invest in yourself.

- Invest in getting professional certificates.

Last, be up to date with current global happenings because these have a direct and massive impact on global economies. If you do not have the time, *make* time. That or you can download newspaper apps and program the tags or keywords that are most relevant to you.

That about covers it for this chapter. Please remember to look at the activity to help you put this into practice. Remember the second chapter about being productive? Now is a good time to do that.

Activity

1. Request your bank statement and look at all your monthly bills. Decide which ones you no longer need and cancel them.

2. For those that you do need, try to negotiate a better deal with your provider or get a better deal elsewhere.

3. Identify a niche in the stock market that you are interested in and make an assessment for possible future investments.

CHAPTER FIVE
FAIL 1,000 TIMES AND THEN
FAIL SOME MORE

"Don't worry if you make mistakes because that's how most people learn." -Alan Sugar (British business magnate, media personality, politician, and political advisor).

Failure is one of the most important steps on a journey that you can make because it allows you to learn. It may feel like things are not going so well. You may want to stop and give up but failing is an incredibly powerful tool to have in your arsenal.

More than half of all small businesses fail within the first year because when they hit a few potholes, they give up. You have to be built for this. You have to have the right mindset. If you don't then you need to develop it.

Imagine if you never failed anything. Wouldn't that be great? Well, no, it wouldn't.

When you continue to do something that you know you'll get right every time, you might make a living from it, but you will become stagnant. Avoiding risks stops you from progressing to new heights. Everyone tends to desire more than they have. You might be thinking, "I'm comfortable in my business," but there is no such thing. Let me explain.

Let's pretend that your perceived level of "comfortable" is earning $45,000 per year. (If you follow the steps within this book, you will reach that figure quickly.) Excellent! However, the more you earn, the more you will want to earn. You'll become accustomed to a certain lifestyle, and then it becomes basic. You're comfortable at $45,000 per year would be a bit more comfortable at $50,000 per year, then $55,000 per year, $65,000, $75,000—it goes on and on.

Doing the same thing, day in and day out, may bring you the success you originally planned for, but with boredom setting in, you will look for ways to get that excitement that you had when you first went into business for yourself. And besides, with you never truly knowing what the future holds, it's always a good idea to keep upping the ante to make sure you will have enough money saved up if times ever get really tight.

A good businessperson is always looking to improve and expand. You would not have picked up this book if you were not an ambitious person. You want to do more, learn more, and earn more. That means one thing—you need to fail more.

It can be a scary concept. After all, it is pretty much hardwired into our brains that failure is a bad thing. But this is a matter of how you see things. You need to change your perspective. Failure can be good or bad; it is on you to determine which one it is.

Together we will look at some common obstacles that would be regarded as failure then see how you can turn these around to become stepping-stones to becoming a better you.

First Scenario

Failure: Your new product line has failed to sell as much as expected. You are out of money and feel that you are at square one.

Response: You now have important information about your market. You know your customer better and have a deeper understanding of what they need. Niche sales have a higher turnover and a more loyal customer base. You have uncovered research that will put you ahead of your competitors, giving you the edge that you need to succeed.

Second Scenario

Failure: Your suppliers did not deliver on time, and you had to cancel an event, which made you look unorganized and untrustworthy.

Response: Having moments where you are weak makes you more relatable to customers. This adds a human element to your business, whereby you become more approachable than mechanical companies. You have also learned valuable lessons about turnaround times and contracts, most likely in the early stages. This means you will not have the same problem in the future when even more business could depend on it. Therefore, in the long run it has saved you money and gained you a more interactive customer base.

Third Scenario

Failure: You took on too many work projects in your excitement, and now you must let some projects go.

Response: You now understand how much your company can handle comfortably. Now you can build on that slowly but surely. And now you will be able to manage your growth and chart your progress.

These are three examples of how failure can be interpreted as a learning curve, a lesson, and a money saver in the long term. Of course, you do not want to approach projects that you *know* will fail. This is different from starting on a project with hope and ambition. Like many things, success is a mindset, and shifting your mind to that positive approach is simpler than you think.

Activity

Think about the time that you failed in the past and analyze what good came from it. Try to do this on a regular basis with your mistakes. Ask yourself what you learned or if there were any other positive outcomes that came along with it. Do this on a regular basis, and your mind will rewire itself to find the positive in everything, to push you forward in all situations.

CHAPTER SIX
GET OUT OF YOUR OWN WAY

Something that we briefly touched on in the last chapter was altering your mindset. One of the most difficult things to do in business is to have self-confidence. You might believe in yourself, your qualifications, your team, or your product, but when reality hits, it is often easy to find excuses.

Excuses are only you blocking you.

They do not offer anything productive to your passion. In this chapter we will discuss the difference between legitimate reasons versus excuses, which come from the internal obstacles blocking you. It may be something you *know* you do, or it could be something you do on a subconscious level. Regardless, you need to address this problem—and you need to address it *now*.

First, let us ask the question: What is a reasonable excuse? The answer to that is simple; there are none.

An excuse is attempting to lessen the blame on you. It is a matter of not taking responsibility. Therefore, it is different than a reason.

A reason is something that is unavoidable, whereas an excuse is something you do to block yourself. A reason could be something like a change that could not be predicted, for example, an occurrence preventing shipment from the distributor for which you have a contract with. That is a reasonable condition to allow you some leeway. This is outside of your control.

An excuse is something you can work around easily but choose not to. In the example with the shipment problem, the reason would be your late delivery. An excuse would be not doing anything about it to meet your customers' demands. It becomes an excuse when you ignore the fact that you could have done something like this:

• Searched for other suppliers during that time

- Arranged a discount because of the inconvenience
- Had a backup plan in case there was a problem with your first supplier

Many of these issues come down to how you approach your business and how you approach yourself. It might sound like some new-age ideology, but self-reflection has many key benefits. Often, we block ourselves out of fear. Knowing what our triggers are can help prevent this. If you know that there is an aspect of the business that you do not like to engage in, you make excuses and put it off. This is not productive or proactive. If you want to stop blocking yourself, as any good businessperson will want to, then you need to learn to work around this. You should address the issue straightaway. By getting things done that you least like doing first, you can remove the anxiety from the rest of your tasks. This is because you won't have the "unwanted" task in the back of your mind because it is already done.

Sometimes however, you must do things in a certain order. This is when it becomes problematic. But there is still no need for excuses. If the thing you do not like doing comes later in the process, you can always outsource the work. Outsourcing is a viable option used by many companies to take the pressure off the workload. It can be used to remove the obstacle that causes you anxiety or stress. Being able to delegate will be a positive step in your development.

Personal development in preventing blockages will also influence your productivity and business. Here are a few exercises you can consider in terms of personal growth:

Open Your Third Eye: With the current world realities, it is imperative to have your third eye open. You need to have open insight, vision, and higher wisdom to free your mind as well as any psychological barriers you may have in your mind. You need to be one with the universe and the vibrations around you. Stay away from all negativity. It can be deeply empowering, which in turn gives you a dramatic increase in self-confidence. This may sound sci-fi, but your intuition and higher wisdom will come alive. This is how you will manifest the life that you want. You will become a new creature.

Adopt a Healthy Lifestyle: It is also important to adopt a healthy lifestyle because eating habits can have significant effects on your business. As the business owner, you are the decision maker, and you must be in the right frame of mind to make healthy decisions for the business. It is a known fact that eating a well-balanced and healthy diet improves your mood, energy, and ability to work. It's also imperative that you get ample amounts of sleep. According to the CDC (Center for Disease Control), getting a good amount of sleep helps the body's blood pressure regulate itself. Exercising is also important. Regular physical activity improves your strength and endurance. And this in turn allows your heart and lungs to have better health, which equates to more energy to tackle the daily entrepreneurial lifestyle. So, why would you not give yourself these little boosts?

Meditate: You can find musical or guided meditation videos on the internet for free. They are an easy and effective way of channeling yourself. There are many apps such as Headspace or Calm that can assist you with this. If you are new to meditation and find it a daunting process, you can search for extremely short versions. There are hundreds of videos on YouTube with three- to five-minute meditational sets. I recommend listening to affirmations while you meditate at first.

Hire Gurus: This may sound like something expensive that only Hollywood celebrities have. The fact is that this is simply not true. There are plenty of people, especially freelancers, who have time in the day to assist you with motivation and blockages. You can find them easily on websites such as Upwork and Fiverr.

Journal: Journaling has proved to be a particularly useful tool for anyone who needs to express their feelings but either doesn't know how or doesn't want to express them to others. Putting words down on paper has been shown to have a therapeutic effect on the mind. It allows the person writing the journal to get all their ideas, concerns, and brain chaos on paper to maybe make sense of what the writer is feeling at that moment. It is especially helpful to do this before bed. Often when doing this, you will find that taking ten minutes before bed gives your subconscious mind room to accommodate new paradigms, and eventually you will awaken your mind to new solutions and experience a refreshed spirit. Gratitude journals have been scientifically proven to reduce long-term anxiety and depression.

Indulge in Holistic Treatments: Reiki, body massages, and aromatherapy are not only relaxing tools for the body but also treatments for the mind as well.

There are also many other kinds of strategies that help with alleviating stress and reforming your mind. Daily affirmations and repeated mantras are extremely useful. Your affirmation could be as simple as "I am going to make today the best it can be for me, my body, my mind, and my business. By enunciating this repeatedly, you will see a positive change.

We are all conditioned, with or without knowing, by elements of our past or our upbringing. So, it comes to a matter of rewiring your brain. Negative situations may cause you to think improperly about the decisions you need to make. This happens on both a personal and business level. In fact, the two are closely interlinked within this chapter. If you want a business to thrive, you must be the dominant force pushing it in that direction—the person saying no to negativity.

Counselors often use cognitive behavioral therapy with their clients; however, it can be a positive aspect of anyone's life. The basic premise is rewiring the brain to see the positive aspects of a negative situation, as we have previously looked at together in this chapter.

"It is possible to get out of your own way, but it requires deliberate attention and careful coordination of many moving parts." — Dave Hollis (CEO of the Hollis Company).

Activity 1

The activity for this chapter is choosing one or more strategies from the list in this chapter and putting them into practice. Give them at least a week to start seeing results.

Activity 2

Think about what it is that you want from your life and your business and where it will take you. Write down a daily affirmation or mantra. Continue to say it aloud. Even better, place it somewhere that you will see it regularly to remind yourself that blockages are temporary, and you have the power to remove them with ease.

CHAPTER SEVEN
TAKE RISKS

Nothing great ever came to those who sat around and did nothing. Greatness comes to those who take *risks*. Would Barack Obama have become the first black president of America if he did not run for office? Would black rights be recognized if it weren't for people like Martin Luther King, Jr., and Malcolm X? Would Larry Ellison be the billionaire co-founder and executive chair and chief technology officer of Oracle Corporation if he didn't take huge risks? Jeff Bezos wouldn't be the richest man in the world if he never took a risk and started Amazon in his garage. It may sound melodramatic to compare yourself to these kinds of people, but there is a powerful business theory called 10x theory. You need to regard yourself with *10x thinking*! This is simply setting your goals ten times greater than what you think you can actually achieve.

I can already sense many of you saying, "But risks are dangerous!" Well, yes! But that's why they are worthwhile. Risks pay rewards. The bigger the risk, the bigger the reward. Here are a few comments on taking risks from the greats:

"Remembering that you are going to die is the best way I know to avoid the trap of thinking you have something to lose. You are already naked. There is no reason not to follow your heart." -Steve Jobs (American business magnate, industrial designer, investor, and media proprietor).

"To win big, you sometimes have to take big risks." - Bill Gates (American business magnate, software developer, investor, and philanthropist).

"Many people are afraid to fail, so they don't try. They may dream, talk, and even plan, but they don't take that critical step of putting their money and their

effort on the line. To succeed in business, you must take risks. Even if you fail, that's how you learn. There has never been, and will never be, an Olympic skater who didn't fall on the ice." -Donald Trump (45th president of the United States, businessman and television personality)

"I don't do nothin' unless I risk humiliating myself and really embarrassing myself. When I have that hanging over my head, it allows me to rise to the occasion."– Mike Tyson (American professional boxer).

You should recognize each one of these highly successful names. These are probably people that you aspire to be like or that you respect. They are also the kind of people you *can* be like.

It's important to understand the balance between a smart risk and a stupid risk. There is no manual that can tell you which risk is a good one. This is something that you'll have to learn. It comes with instinct and is something that every entrepreneur needs to work on. There will be times that the risks don't pay off. If that is something that worries you, then go back to the chapter on failure and reread why you *need* to fail. There's a reminder in there to learn from your failures. The point is that you can't win them all, but the ones you do win will be worth it. In risk taking, every success is a step to a higher level for your business. There is no way that this book can teach you which risks are worth taking. If there was a way to do that, we would all be millionaires, but what this book can offer is a few hints.

- Follow your instinct on what risks to go for.

- If there is time to sleep on it, then do so. Giving yourself that additional pondering time is good for evaluation.

- Never take a risk you can't afford.

- Keep a note of what risks you have taken that have paid off—and the ones that didn't pay.

- Analyze the current state of the market. Something that didn't work before could work in a different market climate.

- Be aware of your customers.

- Create a buyer persona for your customers.

- Look at what your competitors are/are not doing before you make your move. The competition's failures are your learning lessons.

- Always listen to the customer.

That is what you need to do. It might seem like a lot to remember now, but the truth is that it eventually becomes a part of you. In time it becomes like another sense, something you can pull out of the bag at any given moment without a second thought. This is something that you will get used to, and one day you might be the person spinning off inspirational quotes and telling anecdotes about risk to the next generation of entrepreneurs. Take a risk today but keep it smart and keep it calculated.

Activity

This is going to be the longest activity in the book. It is a both a questionnaire and a challenge. The questionnaire is simple; the challenge is acting on it.

- What are you passionate about?

- What are buyers paying for a product in that niche?

- Can you get that product, sell it slightly cheaper, and still make a profit?

- Find a supplier that you can buy it from for a low price.

- How will you market your product to your customers?

- How many products will you be willing to invest in?

- Now do it.

CHAPTER EIGHT
HANG AROUND SUCCESS

Have you ever heard the phrase "like attracts like"? There's a reason for that—it's true. Hanging around with the kind of people you aspire to be like will make you pick up some of their habits and inspire you to go further and push harder.

Think about it this way. If you are on a diet, but you have a friend who constantly eats fast food, you will probably try to avoid them around mealtimes. They would put too much temptation in your way and maybe try to convince you to indulge in their food delights. They would encourage you to be like them because that's comfortable for them. They might question your decisions or even mock them. The same can be said about business mindsets.

It's a sad truth that not everyone will support you, including the people who you were certain would.

Sadly, friends, family, and even your significant other might be one of the things you will lose on your way to becoming successful. But you must press on and continue to elevate. Take the diet example again. Wouldn't it be beneficial to hang out with somebody who wants to join you in healthy activities or go to the gym with you? These are the kind of mindsets you need to add to your circle because investing your time into them is investing in yourself, and after all, that's what good business is all about. You need the kind of person in your life who will push you and not only that but the ones who understand sacrifice and time management.

People who are successful know what it takes. They are the people who have missed their kid's school plays, put in some overtime, and had to miss out on family dinners a few nights. These people have missed birthdays and made so many other sacrifices so that their family's future could be financially secure. These are the people who understand the many sacrifices you have made or will make. Instead of telling you that the jump is too high, they will be the ones showing you the best way to jump off the waterfall, enjoy the leap, and penetrate the water.

Of course, don't miss every special event. But what I am saying is that whatever sacrifices you choose to make; you need to surround yourself with people who understand why you are making them and won't bring negative energy your way about it.

Life is so much easier when supportive people surround you.

Not only that, but you adopt their habits. Good habits are crucial to success! You need to establish the tools to your trade and turn them into habits. That way they become part of your day, especially because you don't need to waste your valuable decision-making time. Steve Jobs famously wore the same black turtleneck, blue jeans, and New Balance sneakers every day. This quickly became his signature look as well as a part of the overall brand of Apple. By having the same outfit each day, that was one less decision he had to make, thereby saving his "battery" for important decisions. This might sound crazy to some people, but that is exactly why you need to hang around successful people—because their actions aren't just habits; they are catalysts for success. By adopting this habit, Steve Jobs became a household name.

Think about all the things you can gain from hanging with rich and successful people, lots.

Being in these circles gets you contacts. You must have heard the adage: "It's not *what* you know but *who* you know." Although this is true, you must still educate yourself in your field of business. We will hone in on education in another chapter. For now, we're going to discuss the "who you know" part. Making contacts is a big part of getting what you need. Associating with these people opens doors for you—doors that they have used themselves at one point in life.

And this applies to all walks of life. Businesses cross over a lot. Imagine that you own a computer company; you might think that a carpenter couldn't help you. Wrong! There is always a chance you might need their services to build computer stands. What you both need, though, is marketing—and there is a huge chance that they will have marketing contacts.

So, say you use their marketing contacts. That contact may have worked with software designers that could support your hardware in a mutually beneficial deal. The chain could be limitless, and you never know how far these links could go.

On the opposite side, once you are established, it is worth associating with young up-and-comers—not only to return the kindness and knowledge you once received, but it may be beneficial to invest in their fresh ideas. Their products might turn into the cash cow every entrepreneur hopes for. Seeing potential is a crucial business skill, and you need to be taking every opportunity to raise your platform. This is also why these rich contacts will be happy to help you as a startup business. One good turn deserves another.

You might be wondering how you meet these people. There are two main ways: in person and online.

In person you could go to events to meet them such as conference halls, country clubs, professional events, seminars, and lectures to name a few. Place yourself in their line of everyday life. Have drinks at upscale establishments, eat at highly rated venues, go to lectures and panel discussions at conventions— most of all, talk to people. Striking up a conversation could be the first step to a million-dollar deal. You never know.

As for meeting successful people online, social media is one of the biggest tools of the decade. It's an easy way to start a conversation. With hashtags it's even easier. Social media marketing is on the rise and will continue to grow. Tagging people, commenting with interesting and strategic content, and spreading positivity is a great way to catch the eye of the circle you want to step into.

Hanging out with people in the lifestyle you aspire to has many perks. They can raise you up, give you motivation, steer you away from slipping off track, introduce healthy habits, make you more productive, and introduce you to the higher-ups. You don't need to abandon everyone around you who doesn't fit the profile, because if they bring positivity to your life, then they are a credit, but adding a little more wealth (both financially and metaphorically) can bring great results.

"If you consistently surround yourself with winners, winning would become the only option in all your endeavors."-Edmond Mbiaka (self-help writer).

You probably have read the power of positive thinking by "Norman Vincent Peale", where he listed series of positive declarations and thoughts that needs to be done daily to create a mental picture of what you want your future to look like.

"Instead of worrying about what you cannot control, shift your energy to what you can create." – Roy T. Bennett, Author of *The Light in the Heart*.

Wealth: You want to be wealthy, right? however, you need to be able to create a mental picture of what this wealth looks like, so as for it to be achievable and not look strange when you eventually achieve your goal and aspirations.

Write down what you want: Part of what it takes to achieve a goal is when you write them down. Writing down your goals means that you can easily visualize them. There is an important correlation between seeing and acting our goals. The probability of being more productive when you pen your goals down is higher than if you don't.

Envision your future: It is important that you also envision your future 20-30years from now. If you find it difficult to do such a long-term envisioning, you can start with about 3-5years (short term) envisioning. You can do this by sitting quietly and think about where and what you want with your life, how things are going, and where you're heading. This is similar to having a self-conversation. Ask yourself a few pointed questions and answer honestly. What are your goals? Are you making progress? Is it working out for you? Does it feel like you're on the right track? Consider those goals realistic after setting them, come up with an execution strategy and **take the first step**

Affirm your desire: Be positive about those goals and reaffirm it on a daily basis, first time when you wake up, reiterate those goals, and see yourself working towards achieving them.

Listen to your inner voice: There is always a voice that says you can do it, as well as another that says you can't achieve it, but you need to listen to the positive voice that says you can't do it. Cancel out the negative thoughts and gut feelings that says you can't do it and listen to the voice that say you can do it. Fight every obstacle on your way to your success.

Take action and transform: It is not enough to proclaim this positively, but to also take the first step and work into transforming your goals into fulfillment.

Hold the vision: Once this comes into reality, make sure you do not deviate from it and do nothing to jeopardize it.

Activity

Here is a long list of things you can do to get in the circles you want to be in. These things can take time. Don't be disheartened—push on. Pick three that you can do in the next seven days.

- Tweet, comment, or vote on a social media post from one of the people you want to be associated with.

- Attend or plan to see a lecture or panel discussion where you can meet like-minded people and build connections.

- Attend a group workshop (or book one) in your chosen field.

- Go for a drink at an upscale bar and strike up a few conversations.

- Go to a business convention and email everyone who gives you a card. You could also give them yours.

- Book or attend a meeting with a business consultant about your next steps, and make sure to check if they have any other clients, they can link you with. Generally, they will do this because they are pleasing two clients and giving added value to their service, which puts them above their competitors

- Email relevant podcasts to see if they have any guest slots and pay them their fee to get your voice out there.

- Do something charitable and make sure it has media coverage (win-win!).

CHAPTER NINE
LIVE BELOW YOUR MEANS

"Just because you can afford it doesn't mean you should buy it." -Suze Orman (American financial advisor, author, and podcast host).

Living below your means might not seem like success, but it is a pathway to get you there. This tends to be a matter of short-term pain for a long-term win. Saving that money to invest in your future now will multiply your funds greatly in future. Regardless if you earn $35,000 or $135,000, you will not achieve financial success without spending less than you earn. Living below your income doesn't mean you can't have nice things. You have to prioritize, get the necessities of life, and postpone any reckless spending. Cutting things out doesn't need to be painful. Here are some things you can do to help save money.

Compare Prices

Whether you're looking to buy car insurance, attain credit cards, get life insurance, refinance a mortgage on a home, or do anything else, there is usually quite a difference between the cheapest and most expensive providers. Because of this, it's worth browsing for the best offers on these services and products to see who can offer you better deals.

Transfer Debt

Consolidate all your small-limit credit cards onto one or two big credit cards so that you will have fewer monthly credit card payments.

Learn to Ask (a Closed Mouth Doesn't Get Fed)

Charisma can get you freebies and better deals. Often you can get a little discount or something for free by asking companies what they can do for long-term customers. Mention better deals with other providers. It might take a little patience, but it is worth it.

Buying in Bulk

Buying in bulk often saves money. This is because the more you buy, the more you save. If you own or manage your own business, it's worth signing up with a wholesaler to see how much money you can save.

Start a Business Account

Often you can save money by starting a business account with a company. There are also many incentives to be had when you start a business account.

Buy to Save

This may sound like a strange statement, but sometimes buying an item to save you in the long run is a better idea. A few examples include better-quality clothes, reusable plastics, contract-free cell phones, and energy-related home improvements. This is also good for the earth.

Purchase Used Items

Purchasing used items can save you a lot of money. Don't be afraid to appear "non-rich," especially when you're on your way to building wealth. It is also good for the earth to buy used items because you won't be using any new raw materials.

Create a Monthly Budget

Making a budget and adhering to it are paramount to reaching a strong financial goal regardless of your financial circumstances. It reduces stress and improves your health because it allows you to take full control of your life. Budgeting is quite important in our everyday financial lives. A budget helps track and control if we are living within our means or if we're overspending. It also helps you channel your funds into where you will get the best returns, stay on top of your bills, and start putting money toward your future goals.

Increase Your Income

There are endless approaches to make more money, but not all of them are viable, and not all of them can be done quickly. Sure, there are some sources for passive income like blogging or writing. But an increase in income can be attained only through an increase in productivity, and you can do this by devoting the right amount of time on important endeavors while living below your earning.

Don't Try to Impress the Neighbors

You need to live your life for you rather than living your life for others. It's important to restrict your spending on the things you like and value instead of living extravagantly to impress others.

Do not succumb to the internal pressure of society by wasting your hard-earned cash buying things to impress strangers.

"People who live far below their means enjoy a freedom that people busy upgrading their lifestyles can't fathom."– Naval Ravikant (co-founder, chairman, and former CEO of AngelList).

Activity 1

Check what you can remove or alter comfortably from your regular expenses and act on it.

Activity 2

Make a list of your all your bills (insurance, phone, internet service provider, etc.) and try to find alternative providers that you might save money with.

CHAPTER TEN
EDUCATE YOURSELF

Education is an important part of success. Education is the process of facilitating learning or the acquisition of knowledge, skills, values, beliefs, and habits. So therefore, educating yourself about your business and about your market will help you spring to success.

"Education is the passport to the future, for tomorrow belongs to those who prepare for it today." -Malcolm X (African American minister, civil rights activist, and supporter of black nationalism).

To achieve anything, you need to be educated about it. Things rarely fall in the laps of those with little understanding, and when they do, there's usually someone behind them who is educated and calling the shots.

Business is a game of knowledge. Therefore, investing in your education is a fantastic way to invest in your success. It is of the utmost importance to invest in knowledge and update your skills. Learn new things daily from reading, mentors, and successful stories. Apply for an online business course, attend seminars, buy business and investment books written by experts, or try anything else along those lines. Any time you are taking tried and tested knowledge and committing it to memory, you are investing well in your business.

Beyond these, it is also a good idea to invest in yourself by reading books on personal development. This is one of the most important investments you can make for your financial future.

If the economy crashed, you lost your investments, your business lost all its clients, and you lost all your assets, your business would come to a stop. However, with the proper education you will be able to bounce right back—you will always have an edge. You need to invest in yourself, diversify, and sharpen your skills. Start reading books like *The Secret* (by Rhonda Byrne), *Rich Dad Poor Dad* (by Robert Kiyosaki), *Make Your Own Damn Cheese: Understanding, Navigating, and Mastering the 3 Mazes of Success* (John A. Chuback), and *Hustle Harder, Hustle Smarter* (by Curtis "50 Cent" Jackson). These are important to help you become a better you.

Educating yourself and your staff is crucial. You need to educate yourself on your market. You need to delve deep into what your customer base is, what they want, how they access it, what they are willing to pay, and what the current trends are. Trends can change seemingly overnight. Look back at the last twenty years with fidget spinners, the slinky, and beanie babies. You need to be able to zero in on these trends and act on them before they lose momentum. This is where education on your market comes in.

Beyond this, educating yourself on *how* to market is also important. You need to know who to target. If you want to market a children's toy, you decide whether to cater to the parent or child. Each would be a significantly different process. This is where your market understanding can help.

You also need to educate yourself on legalities. This may sound dull, but it is incredibly important. For instance, if you work internationally, you need to know the legislation between borders. For example, some preservatives banned in the United Kingdom are legal in the United States. Trying to ship foods containing theses preservatives could result in severe lawsuits being filed. This could potentially have catastrophic consequences. If it goes on long enough, it could close your business.

You need to educate yourself about yourself. That may seem like a weird statement, but one of the best ways to get better is to first figure out where you're starting. Do a SWOT analysis. It may be worth writing things down such as "I need a break to recharge my batteries after four days" or "I work best in the afternoon." Once you have this information, you can put it to good use, scheduling yourself for success.

A few things that you could do on a daily basis to educate yourself are: listening to educational podcasts, reading books, keeping up with the news, looking at competitors' products, checking in with your team and customers, watching documentaries, and speaking to people in your field. These are easy tasks that you can do. They may seem like nothing at all, but among them all, they will add up to something great—like a grain of sand in a clam shell that eventually becomes a pearl.

What Is the Wheel of Life?

The Wheel of Life is a basic but powerful tool that helps you visualize all the essential areas of your life at once. It is frequently used by life coaches and career coaches to give their clients a bird's-eye view of their lives. By looking at a visual and pictorial representation of all the areas of your life at once, the wheel helps you better comprehend which of your life areas are flourishing and which need the most work.

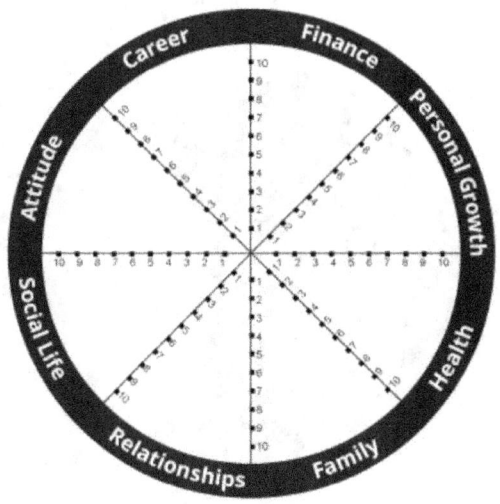

The Wheel of Life

A Venn diagram is an illustration that uses circles to show the relationships among things or finite groups of things. Circles that overlap have a commonality, whereas circles that do not overlap do not share those traits. Venn diagrams visually represent the similarities and differences between two concepts.

STEPS TO ACHIEVING THE BUSINESS WE WANT

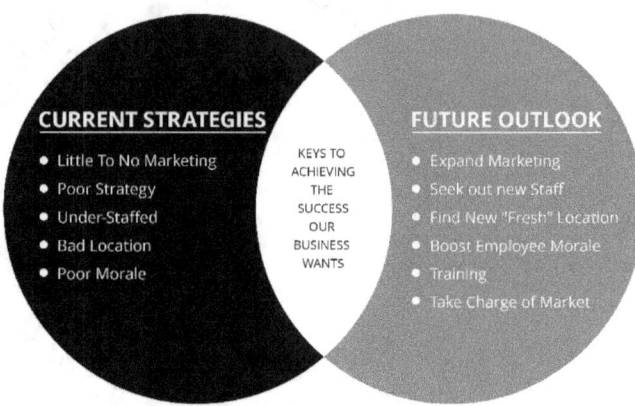

CURRENT STRATEGIES

- Little To No Marketing
- Poor Strategy
- Under-Staffed
- Bad Location
- Poor Morale

KEYS TO
ACHIEVING
THE
SUCCESS
OUR
BUSINESS
WANTS

FUTURE OUTLOOK

- Expand Marketing
- Seek out new Staff
- Find New "Fresh" Location
- Boost Employee Morale
- Training
- Take Charge of Market

Venn Diagram

"Who questions much, shall learn much, and retain much." -Francis Bacon (English philosopher and statesman).

Activity

Do a SWOT analysis for your business, and then do a
SWOT for yourself.

CHAPTER ELEVEN
KEEP YOUR MONEY WORKING

"If you do not find a way to make money while you sleep, you will work until you die."– Warren Buffet (American investor, business tycoon, philanthropist, and CEO and chairman at Berkshire Hathaway).

As Warren Buffet said, you need to find a way to make your money work for you, or else you will work till you die. How scary and real is that? Who does not want to rest in their old age? Of course, we all want to do so. It is therefore imperative to find a balance between spending and investing to start earning passive incomes.

Purchasing items that accrue interest is the best move to make. These items can be purchased and liquidated later (if need be). These are items that are less likely to lose value, and when and if they lose value, it's only by a small margin. These items can be sold during hard times. They include items such as collectibles, antiques, property portfolios, or gold. Of course, the best options are often the ones that make you money while still holding value, like real estate or hotels that you can rent out. What follows are points that need to be considered if you want your money to work for you.

1.   Get a Financial Advisor/Planner

You need to get someone who has a lot of experience with money. You need to talk to this person, and hopefully they can help guide you financially.

They are experts in giving financial advice. Getting a good financial planner is a crucial step on your way to financial freedom.

When you schedule your first meeting with your advisor/planner, here are some questions you might want to ask:

- How do you set short-, medium-, and long-term financial goals?

- How do you set strategies to help achieve these goals?

- How do you create a monthly budget and an investment plan?

- What are your investment options?

2. **Invest in the Stock Market**

There are several companies or stocks you can invest in today. We now have apps that can give suggestions of stocks to invest in. These apps can also give insights into past trends and projections of these stocks, so you do not need to be a financial expert before investing. You also do not need a huge sum of money to start investing. Apps such as Acorns, Stash, and Robinhood can help even newbies get into investing.

3.   **Invest in Products**

Products can electrify your passive income. Buy products for a low price, then turn around, and repackage them to sell for profit. For instance, you can invest $175 to buy 100 T-shirts at $1.75. Inscribe your logo for $500, at $5 per shirt, and with an initial $25 fee, that comes to $525. The total investment for the T-shirts stands at $700.

Based on this example, the cost price for each T-Shirt is $7.00. You can decide to sell each shirt at $20. By the time you sell off the 100 T-shirts, you would have grossed $2,000 ($20 x 100 T-shirts). By the time you subtract $700 (the invested amount), you've made a net profit of $1,300.

Now you have two options: you either reinvest that same $700 or double it and make a $1,400 investment, leaving you with $600 profit, or you can invest almost the whole $2,000 by buying 280 shirts at $1.75 (you may even get a further discount based on more volume), coming to a total of $490. Your printing costs for 280 shirts will be $1,400. Repeat these steps, and you get a $5,600 gross with a net profit of $3,710.

Keep flipping your money, and $5,000 will turn to $10,000; $10,000 will turn to $20,000; $20,000 will turn to $30,000; $30,000 will turn to $40,000 and so on and so forth.

4.   Contribute to a 401k or IRA

401Ks/IRAs are tax-advantaged investment accounts in which your money is wisely invested for greater returns. Investment in these vehicles is a good way of making your money efficiently work for you.

5.   Use Alternative Passive Income Streams

Another way to earn passive income is with alternative passive income streams. There are several investment options to dive into that give passive income: affiliate marketing, drop shipping, cost-per-click (CPC) ads, display ads, Airbnb, starting a YouTube channel, real estate investment trusts (REITs), peer-to-peer lending, and annuities.

6.   **Take Advantage of a High-Yield Savings Account**

Typically, saving accounts give as low as 0.1% interest per annum on your savings. However, it is beneficial to open high-yielding saving accounts where you can earn as much as 5% on your savings. This is usually the case with online banks that have low overhead costs. It is also noteworthy that these banks have limitations on the number of times you can withdraw money monthly. The more money you have in the bank, the better: $1 million in one of these accounts will provide you with a yearly salary of $50,000!

7.   Know the Difference between Good Debt versus Bad Debt

At some point in our lives, we have reasons to go in debt. It may seem like a way of life; however, if you are going to be in debt, choose good debt, not bad debt. Good debt increases your net worth or has future value, for example, borrowing to buy into real estate, gold, and so on, for future resale. In contrast, bad debts are debts that plunge you into further debts. They are spent on items that hold no future value. So, if you go in debt, make sure its good debt.

8.   **Join a Credit Union**

Credit unions are outperforming big banks and gaining members at an exponential rate. Credit unions are owned by its members, and they are operated by the people in the community that also happen to be members. Their whole reason for being is to assist the financial wellness of their members. They make returns to their "member owners" in the form of lower fees, lower interest rates, more services, and higher dividends on deposits. Profits from big banks, however, are funneled into expensive national advertising budgets and huge executive compensation packages. Credit unions are also a more personalized way of handling your finances. And because your relationship with the credit union actually grows and gets better with time, you'll have better chances at securing a personal or small business loan. Deposits at credit unions are insured by the NCUA (National Credit Union Administration). According to surveys, credit unions are the most trusted segment of the financial services industry. Memberships are open to anyone who wants to join, and the benefits begin immediately. You should have a personal and business account at a credit union. Even though credit unions are a better choice, big banks still serve their purpose so have an account there as well.

As you can see, there are many ways to manage your money and make it work for you. Which way you choose depends on your situation as well as your goals. Look to the future and picture exactly how you want your life to end up. Now what steps above do you think will help you achieve your goals? Implement as many steps as you want. Now let's keep our money working!

Activity

Read these steps again, decide which of them (select at least three) works best for you, and begin to act on each one.

A FINAL NOTE

Thank you for investing in this book, but most of all, thank you for investing in yourself. You have now reached the end and can now carve out a successful future for your business and for yourself. If you take note of everything you have read, and stay mindful and vigilant, then you are well on your way to your goals.

All that is left is for you to begin. Remember the mantra you wrote for yourself, and always be focused on what this dream means to you. Be happy and healthy as you fill your life with all the things you deserve, as you work toward your goals. In everything you do, be passionate and show the world who you are and who you are going to be. Remember that some risks pay off, contacts are invaluable, and at the heart of this journey is one person. That person is you.

This book will be here for you to reference at any time. Until then, get out there, get working, and pour your soul and passion into everything you do—in business and in your personal life.

"Our deepest fear is not that we are inadequate. Our deepest fear is that we are powerful beyond measure. It is our light, not our darkness that most frightens us. We ask ourselves, 'Who am I to be brilliant, gorgeous, talented, fabulous?' Who are you not to be? You are a child of God. Your playing small does not serve the world. There's nothing enlightened about shrinking so that other people won't feel insecure around you. We are all meant to shine, as children do. We were born to make manifest the glory of God that is within us. It's not just in some of us; it's in everyone. And as we let our own light shine, we unconsciously give other people permission to do the same. As we are liberated from our own

fear, our presence automatically liberates others." – Marianne Williamson (American author, spiritual leader, politician, and activist).

www.ingramcontent.com/pod-product-compliance
Lightning Source LLC
Chambersburg PA
CBHW070357220526
45467CB00001B/416